Advising Success: Lessons from American Military Assistance Efforts since World War II

A Monograph
by
Major Bryan K. Batson
Field Artillery

School of Advanced Military Studies
United States Army Command and General Staff College
Fort Leavenworth, Kansas

AY 2011-002

Abstract

ADVISING SUCCESS: LESSONS FROM AMERICAN MILITARY ASSISTANCE EFFORTS SINCE WORLD WAR II, by Major Bryan K. Batson, United States Army, 52 pages.

The Global War on Terror brought about several military assistance efforts that include the training and development of foreign security forces. The United States has been providing advisors to foreign security forces around the world for over 120 years. Security force advising maintains a long history within U.S. doctrinal discussions on key components of developing safe and secure environments. Recent changes in military advising doctrine resulted from efforts to make modern military advising more effective. Analysis of multiple cases from the U.S. advisory experience shows that successful advisory efforts share some common approaches. Regardless of the size of the mission, four factors trend toward success when applied in advisory efforts. The advisor needs to account for local political and cultural limitations on the overall effort. The location of the training area needs to provide the ability to minimalize interactions between the host nation's population and the advisors and the elements receiving assistance. The advisory effort needs to include professionalization of other security forces inside a state beyond just the military. Finally, the duration of the mission and the term of individual assignments need to provide the ability to maintain long-term relationships between the advisors and their counterparts.

Table of Contents

Introduction

Advising foreign forces is as old as the written history of warfare itself. In order to increase capacity, states seek out allies and when necessary train their allied forces to perform alongside, or in lieu of, the state's own military. Thucydides' *History of the Peloponnesian War* provides one of the earliest historical examples of this action when he explains how Sparta prepared Syracuse for war with Athens by sending the general Gylippus to organize, train, and lead them.[1] History contains many examples of one nation assisting another in the development of a professional military. Indeed, the utility of military assistance for partner nations through advisory efforts remains a critical element of the United States global engagement strategy. The current and longstanding doctrine of the military of the United States when conducting military assistance to a partner country, in conjunction with efforts to maintain a safe and secure environment in that state, incorporates a spectrum of interagency support. The doctrine states the intent to use the whole of government approach.[2] Building up another nation's security forces, whether as part of the nation's foreign policy engagement and/or in post-conflict situations, often falls on the military to execute.

U.S. Army doctrine clearly stipulates that military advising, as a component of the larger function of security force assistance, is a core competency of what the U.S. Army does.[3] General Martin E. Dempsey reiterated this policy in his introduction to Field Manual 3-07.1 *Security Force Assistance*.[4] This is strongly reflects in the number and scope of advisory missions the U.S. executed during the course of its history. Advising foreign indigenous forces was important to the

---

[1] Thucydides, *History of the Peloponnesian War* (London: Penguin Books, 1972), 470.

[2] Department of Defense, Joint Publication (JP) 3-57 *Civil-Military Operations* (Washington D.C.: Government Printing Office, July 2008), IV-2.

[3] Department of Defense, *Department of Defense Directive Number 3000.05* (Washington D.C.: Government Printing Office, November 28, 2005), 2.

[4] Department of the Army, Field Manual (FM) 3-07.1 *Security Force Assistance* (Washington D.C.: Government Printing Office, 2009), 1.

United States successes in many regions around the globe. The 2010 *Quadrennial Defense Review* recognized that "sustaining existing alliances and creating new partnerships are central elements of U.S. security strategy."[5] As the Army continues to develop its doctrine to the realities of the current geopolitical environment and predict those missions that are likely to occur in the future, it remains imperative to retain the models, practices and procedures of the past that have work well.

The American experience with military advising and security force assistance dates back at least one-hundred and twenty years. Discounting operations training Native Americans for militarily use against other tribes or as local police forces on reservations, the first formal advisory effort the U.S. participated in followed the Spanish American War.[6] The multiple advising experiences of the U.S. ran through the twentieth century and continue today. Pre-World War I through the Interwar period saw American advisory missions in its overseas possessions with a large effort in the Philippines, in the Far East, and especially in Latin American countries.[7] Uncomfortable with its own empire, the U.S. Government struggled with articulating the policies it was pursuing. The guiding principle behind the interventions in the western hemisphere became the Monroe Doctrine, and Roosevelt's Corollary to the Monroe Doctrine. In reference to struggling Latin American states Robert Lansing, Woodrow Wilson's Secretary of State, wrote a

---

[5] Department of Defense, *Quadrennial Defense Review Report* (Washington D.C.: Department of Defense, February 2010), 57.

[6] Richard L. Millett, *Searching for Stability: the Development of U.S. Constabulary Forces in Latin America and the Philippines.* The Long War Series Occasional Paper 30. (Fort Leavenworth, KS: Combat Studies Institute Press, 2010), 1.

[7] Some examples of U.S. advisory efforts since the Spanish-American War include: Cuba (1898-1902 and 1906-1909), The Philippines (1899-1913 and 1933-1954) , China (1900-1901, and 1945-1949), Mexico (1916-17), Russia (1917-1918), Panama (1918-1920, 1946-1984), Greece (1945-1949), Indochina (1945-1954), South Korea (1945-1954), Japan (1945-1950), Lebanon (1958), Viet Nam (1955-1975), Laos (1957-1975), Guatemala (1960-present), Thailand (1961-present), Colombia (1962-Present), Dominican Republic (1965-19676), El Salvador (1981-1992), Honduras (1983-1989), Afghanistan (2001-present), Georgia (2002-2007), Iraq (2003-present), Palestinian Authority (2008-2010). This list is not all inclusive.

memo stating, "It is necessary for the national safety of the United States … that it aid the people of those republics in establishing and maintaining honest and responsible governments to such extent as may be necessary in each particular case."[8] The ultimate aim of all advisory efforts throughout the U.S. experience focused on the establishment of stable governments that cooperated with the United States on the global stage.

After World War II, the United States pursued an expanded role on the world stage. Confrontation with perceived Soviet Union expansionist policies during the Cold War prompted the dispatch of advisory missions around the globe. Immediately after the war, there was a need to train constabulary forces in areas under direct military occupation, including Italy, Germany, and Japan. By 1947, the United States stepped into Britain's traditional sphere of influence in the Eastern Mediterranean, undertaking military assistance and advising efforts in Greece and Turkey. During the Cold War, South Korea typified a large advisory mission with military and constabulary policing functions. El Salvador provides a case were a limited small-scale advisory force executed a successful mission under restrictive political limitations. As extremes of large and small advisory missions during the Cold War, these two examples provide a good source to highlight the commonality in the U.S. models despite being much different in their application.

The end of the Cold War did not bring an end to American military advising. On the contrary, security force advising continues unabated, in many different nations worldwide under differing circumstances and with differing outcomes.[9] Some advisory missions changed as the Cold War ended. Others reached their desired outcome and concluded successfully. Still others began after the Cold War either as a result of new partnership agreements, or due to the

---

[8]Robert Lansing, "Memorandum by Secretary of State Robert Lansing for President Woodrow Wilson, November 24, 1915," *Papers Relating to the Foreign Affairs of the United States: The Lansing Papers,* Vol. II (Washington, DC: Government Printing Office, 1940), 466.

[9]Robert D. Ramsey III, *Advising Indigenous Forces: American Advisors in Korea, Vietnam, and El Salvador.* The Long War Series Occasional Paper 18, (Fort Leavenworth, KS: Combat Studies Institute Press, 2006), 2.

emergence of military conflict. Examples of a new partnership include Georgia and Azerbaijan two former Soviet Republics that sought out U.S. assistance after the fall of the Soviet Union. Military conflicts led to U.S. military assistance in Bosnia, Saudi Arabia, and Kuwait. The Global War on Terror added even more nations to the list of those receiving military assistance from the U.S., including Iraq, Afghanistan, and the Philippines to list a few .[10] An example of a mission that grew, shrank, and evolved from its Cold War origins into a unique program during the current period is that of Colombia. Columbia experienced tremendous political infighting and politically inspired violence through the 19th and 20th centuries. The emergence of a communist insurgency in the 1960s drew the initial small and military oriented advisory effort. The lack of state control over much of the Colombia's interior allowed for the development of criminal drug cartels that threatened the power of the central government even further. U.S. military assistance to Colombia expanded I the 1980s and 1990s to deal with the criminal threat. By 2001 the effort had morphed again to include a comprehensive counter-terrorism, counter-narcotics, and counter-insurgency composite mission. The change in international relations from a bipolar system through America's unipolar moment, to a more diverse multipolar world, increases rather than decreases the possible nations that the U.S. potentially could support with a military assistance mission and advisory effort.

All of these advisory missions from the early era of American expansion in the Philippines, through the Cold War, to the modern era affect the use of U.S. advisory forces today and in the future. This paper examines three case studies of successful military advisory missions from various eras of U.S. assistance efforts. The monograph highlights common factors from successful large and small military advisory efforts throughout U.S. history that are well suited for application in the current Global War on Terrorism. The methodology of the research is to

---

[10] Donald Stoker, "The History and Evolution of Foreign Military Advising and Assistance, 1815-2007," in *Military Advising and Assistance: From Mercenaries to Privatization, 1815-2007*, by Donald Stoker, ed. (New York, NY: Routledge, 2008), 7.

examine each of the three cases for multiple factors including the political, cultural, and social interactions between advisors, client security forces, and host nation population, as well as scope, size, and duration of mission. Where the data exists, examination of the cultural training and typical length of service for advisors is a factor for consideration. The impacts of cultural training and the increased understanding of the operating environment resulting from extending the duration of missions deserve examination. Investigation of these three cases shows that military advisory and assistance efforts that account for local political and cultural limitations, minimize the visible public interaction between advisors and host nation personnel, include professionalization of other security forces beyond just the military, and rely on trainers with extended exposure and expertise with the host nation tend towards success.

The cases considered for this research include advisory missions in South Korea, El Salvador, and Colombia spanning half of the 120 years of U.S. military assistance to other nations. Each of these three missions had unique political and cultural limitations that affected the advisory effort. As a result, the model design of each assistance effort differed from case to case. Each of these three efforts was successful to varying degrees.[11] The three cases span a range in size, complexity, and historical timeframe. The cases studied all achieved the end state pursued by the U.S. While studying unsuccessful efforts could be useful and provide counterpoints, this study is intentionally limited to successful efforts for the purpose of focus in comparison.

_____

[11] In these cases each met the objectives set by the U.S. In South Korea, a military and police force capable of securing the country in the face of the Communist threat resulted from U.S. advisory efforts. In El Salvador, after an initial assessment of the issues behind the insurgency, the U.S. opted to use a small effort (55 personnel) to professionalize Salvadorian forces to the point they could successfully withstand the Farabundo Marti para Liberacion Nacional (FMLN) and achieve a political settlement to end the insurgency. Colombia proved an interesting case due to its changes in desired outcomes. Over the life of the ongoing effort in Colombia, the advisory effort transitioned from a counter-communist insurgency, to a counter-narcotics mission, and finally to a composite of counter-insurgency and counter-narcotics. Though the Colombian effort is still ongoing, in each phase it achieved its objectives and forced a change on the opposition.

Given the changing terminology pertinent to advising efforts over time, it is necessary to review some key terms used in this paper. Over the century and a half of the American experience with training foreign security forces, definitions used to codify the process went through periods of vogue, only to be replacement later by some neologism. Some terms remain consistent, but most ebb and flow in usage throughout the period examined. Counterinsurgency operations as an example is a contemporary term meaning all of the political, economic, social, and military actions taken by a government for the purpose of suppression of insurgent, resistance, and revolutionary movements.[12] The concept derives its place in American military lexicon from the U.S. Civil War and the era of Reconstruction. It derives from a similar term of that era, counter-guerrilla warfare. Guerrillas and its modern derivative insurgent refer to irregular combatants not regulated by an established military authority or international convention of war.[13] The military as a rule has two roles in counterinsurgency: combat, generally counter-guerrilla in nature, and pacification.

Where counter-guerrilla is combat related, pacification includes civil, administrative and constabulary functions required to establish and maintain government authority.[14] Military governance subsumed that part of the pacification including the civil and administrative functions of a state when performed by an occupying military during World War II. After falling out of common usage in the first half of the 20th century, pacification became vogue during the Vietnam conflict. A subsidiary activity of pacification is the development of a constabulary. A constabulary in refers to officers of the peace organized in a military basis. Contextually it is a

[12] Andrew J. Birtle, *U.S. Army Counterinsurgency and Contingency Operations Doctrine 1860-1941* (Washington D.C.: United States Army Center of Military History, 2003), 3.

[13] Andrew J. Birtle, *U.S. Army Counterinsurgency and Contingency Operations Doctrine 1942-1979* (Washington D.C.: United States Army Center of Military History, 2007), 4.

[14] Ibid, 4.

militarized police force.[15] Constabulary forces were vogue in the American West during the Indian Wars and through the Spanish-American War and the pacification of the Philippines. The Allies also used them in Post-World War II Korea, but eventually the constabulary forces they created became a functional part of the Republic of Korea Army.

Another term important in the context of counterinsurgency is "small wars" or those conflicts that focus on partisans and regular forces engaging in limited, small unit actions. Small wars as a term originates in Napoleonic European warfare, but resumed importance in describing U.S. actions in Latin America during the first half of the 20th century.[16] Small wars as a term was popular within the U.S. Marine Corps in the interwar period, fell out of vogue and then reemerged in the 1990s. Low intensity conflict, referred to as LIC, became popular terminology during the 1960s to address counterinsurgency, and internal defense and development. Internal defense included those actions taken to protect a society from subversion, lawlessness, and insurgency, while internal development involved strengthening the roots, functions, and capabilities of government.[17] Stability operations and stability and support operations are also synonymous derivatives of counterinsurgency and LIC that achieved inclusion in doctrine between the late 1960s and the late 1990s. Military assistance in a similar nature is the modern equivalent of internal defense and development. It includes military aid programs of equipment, spare parts, and financial assistance to foreign nations partnered with the United States as well as the training, advising and support not only in using the equipment provided through military aid, but also in professionalizing the force and facilitating reforms that overcome the root cause of

---

[15] Birtle, *U.S. Army Counterinsurgency...1860-1941*, 58.

[16] Ibid, 15-16.

[17] Birtle, *U.S. Army Counterinsurgency...1942-1976*, 420-421.

insurgencies.[18] This paper focuses on the advisory effort itself as a crucial subcomponent of military assistance.

A sizable volume of written material exists on the subject of advising, with an increase in frequency occurring in the last decade. Each case has its own pool of related material as well. The Korean case has the largest volume of research material available. El Salvador and Colombia are much less investigated cases on the whole. The Colombian case is particularly short on data concerning the counterinsurgency advisory mission, though useful data on the counter-narcotics advising mission is available. The volume of material available for researching the cases included: military doctrinal manuals, materials covering the general principles of military assistance and advising, detailed histories of the cases in question, compilations of shorter studies of multiple cases intended to show trends through time and/ or locations, and works that tend to be individual narratives of specific aspects of each case.

The existing body of literature includes doctrinal manuals such as Joint Publication 3-57, *Civil-Military Operations* that define the nature of military advising, the scope and structure of the mission including how it fits into the greater civil-military operations construct and how to plan and coordinate actions inside a host nation. The principle doctrinal manual concerning military advising for the Army is Field Manual (FM) 3-07.1, *Security Force Assistance*. This manual explains in detail the methodology, structure and rationale of the current advisory model. While the current model of Advise and Assist Brigades (AABs) does not match historic models, it provides a key point of reference to determine if best practices from enduring trends in security force assistance bear out in current operations.[19] The utility of FM 3-07.1 is that it "addresses common characteristics and considerations for conducting security force assistance and clarifies

---

[18] Ibid, 167.

[19] Department of the Army. *Field Manual (FM) 3-07.1 Security Force Assistance* (Washington D.C.: Government Printing Office, 2009), 4-1.

8

what units and individual advisors must understand to work "by, with, and through" their counterparts."[20] FM 3-07.10, *Advising: Multi-service Tactics, Techniques, and Procedures for Advising Foreign Forces* reinforces FM 3-07.1 by providing detailed guidance on how advisors execute missions within the context of security force assistance. Paul Mark's article "Joint Pub 3-07.15, Tactics, Techniques and Procedures for Advising Foreign Nationals and the American Mission" provides an insightful analysis of gaps in doctrine on military assistance and the perception of bias against advisors in the public, the government, and the military.[21] Written at the beginning of the Global War on Terror, Mark's work points out existing gaps in the doctrine on advising, and attempts to explain the conditions when the judicious application of advisors could reduce the need to commit large numbers of troops.

Beyond doctrine or analysis of doctrine, books and articles on lessons learned from history provide application for how advisors can execute their mission with the highest probability for success. Robert D. Ramsey III provided a useful compilation on the nature of advising with *Advise for Advisors: Suggestions and Observations from Lawrence to the Present.* From T.E. Lawrence's personal conclusions on how to be an effective advisor through the lessons learned by American advisors in Vietnam, El Salvador, and Iraq to a RAND study on advisor-counterpart interactions, Ramsey's work provides the compendium of key factors for developing successful advisors.

Andrew J. Birtle provides the most comprehensive view of the doctrine behind the U.S. Army's official policy on military assistance in his two-volume work *U.S. Army Counterinsurgency and Contingency Operations Doctrine 1860-1941* and U.S. *Army Counterinsurgency and Contingency Operations Doctrine 1942-1976*. These two works cover the

---

[20] Ibid, 1.

[21] Paul Marks, "Joint Pub 3-07.15, Tactics, Techniques and Procedures for Advising Foreign Nationals and the American Mission," *Small Wars and Insurgencies* (Spring 2001), 32-33.

origin, history, and permutation of terminology arising from the competition of ideas and politics that drive the counterinsurgency debate. His intellectual history dispels many of the myths concerning the perceived lack of consideration given to guerrilla warfare and nation building in the history of American military doctrine. In meticulous fashion, he shows that the modern idea of counterinsurgency lies at the end of a long train of U.S. thought that directly reflects the impacts of military operation beginning with the U.S. Civil War. He shows that the history of the counterinsurgency era that took place between World War II and the end of the Vietnam War validated some enduring concepts such as increased education, economic development, and social reforms as critical to success, while exposing some of the failures of misguided or unattainable political and social policy.[22]

Military Advising and Assistance: From Mercenaries to Privatization, 1815-2007 edited by Donald Stoker provides a series of essays that trace the history of military advising from Egypt in 1815 to Iraq in the modern day. Furthermore, it projects how the current trends are likely to change in the future. This compilation begins with Stoker's own history of advising article "The History and Evolution of Foreign Military Advising and Assistance, 1815-2007" highlighting six categories of advising. He maintains that advisory missions generally exist for modernization, nation building, penetration, ideology, counter-insurgency, or profit.[23] The rest of the work consists of 12 detailed case studies and a final chapter warning of the trend of private, corporate, military advising for profit. One of the most concise amalgamations of advisor techniques across multiple missions is John D. Waghelstein's "Ruminations of a Wooly Mammoth, or Training and Advising in Counterinsurgency and Elsewhere During the Cold War." This work tracks the enduring principles learned by Waghelstein between 1962 and 1987 advising forces for two tours

---

[22] Birtle, *U.S. Army Counterinsurgency...1942-1976,* 495.

[23] Donald Stoker, "The History and Evolution of Foreign Military Advising and Assistance, 1815-2007." In *Military Advising and Assistance: From Mercenaries to Privatization, 1815-2007,* Donald Stoker, ed. (New York, NY: Routledge, 2008), 2.

in Vietnam and five tours in various Central American countries. Critical advisor lessons learned in multiple efforts include keeping the U.S. profile small so the client will do the job, which enables providing help from the background.[24] Smaller U.S. footprints force the host nation to take responsibility for their own insurgencies.[25] Advisory efforts should also include police forces because "police forces have a better feel for what is happening on the street or in the countryside than the military does."[26] Waghelstein ultimately advises that even enduring principles have to be "tweaked to fit each unique situation" because culture matters.[27] The principle conclusions from the complete collection of essays show that the military advising between nations is an expanding trend. The security training market is associated to globalization and reforms of the private as well as security sector. The essays together show a slow trend to transition from wholly militarily run advisor programs to those that rely on private security firms with many associated risks and opportunities.

Former Deputy Assistant Secretary of Defense for Policy and Planning Dr. Thomas G. Mahnken provides a discussion of recent policy on the role and utility of advisory efforts. He articulates the role of military advisors as a key component of the U.S. indirect strategy to defeat terrorist extremist groups. His essay "The Role of Advisory Support in the Long War Against Terrorist Extremist Groups" examines the debate on the issue, fleshes out a strategy for U.S developing military advisory efforts, and recommends areas for future research on the issue. Mahnken scopes out a future for "The Long War" that requires American forces to execute operations as part of a long term, low visibility, complex operations in areas of the world where

---

[24] John D. Waghelstein, "Ruminations of a Wooly Mammoth, or Training and Advising in Counterinsurgency and Elsewhere during the Cold War." in *Military Advising and Assistance: From Mercenaries to Privatization, 1815-2007*, Donald Stoker, ed. (New York, NY: Routledge, 2008), 157.

[25] Ibid, 164.

[26] Ibid, 166.

[27] Ibid, 166-167.

U.S. forces do not traditionally operate.[28] He focuses on the essential advisory efforts underway in Iraq and Afghanistan, stating that they are the most relevant models for the way ahead, rather than historical models found in places like the Philippines and Thailand.[29] He fundamentally stresses that the key to success can be found in T.E. Lawrence's injunction to "not do too much with our own hands" and that local clients should provide solutions to the problems in their own way in order to achieve lasting solutions.[30]

Since the start of the Global War on Terror, and especially since 2005 the volume of graduate school dissertations, theses, and monographs written on the topic of advising foreign forces as a component of a successful counterinsurgency effort rose dramatically. A similar spike in scholarly research on the topic occurred in conjunction with the Vietnam War. Several recent monographs from the School of Advanced Military studies influenced the analysis behind this paper. Two of the most influential monographs on the writing of this paper include Lieutenant Colonel David S. Pierce's "Training and Advising Foreign Militaries: We have Done This Before", and Major John D. Tabb's "The Korean Military Advisory Group (KMAG): A Model for Success?" From the Army War College, James S. Corum's monograph "Training Indigenous Forces in Counterinsurgency: A Tale of Two Insurgencies" provided useful insight. The Command and General Staff College MMAS monograph for William C. Taylor "The U.S. Army and Security Force Assistance: Assessing the Need for an Institutionalized Advisory Capability" also proved useful. Based on the historical model, it is likely that as the Global War on Terror decreases in scale of forces committed to the advising mission, a similar drop will occur in the volume of research done on advising.

---

[28] Thomas G. Mahnken, "The Role of Advisory Support in the Long War Against Terrorist Extremist Groups", in *Security Assistance: U.S. and International Perspectives*, Kendall D. Gott and Michael G. Brooks, eds., 505-518, (Fort Leavenworth, KS: Combat Studies Institute Press, 2006), 506.

[29] Ibid, 507.

[30] Ibid, 508.

From T.E. Lawrence to the present, the written history and lessons learned from advising foreign forces generates models for the continued success of military assistance. Doctrine and personal experience from many authors capture the enduring principles of advising from the individual traits required in an advisor, to the organization and techniques of successful efforts. These enduring lessons and models provide operational lessons for the future of military advising. With the current geopolitical environment of revolutions throughout the Middle East, the ongoing Global War on Terror, the continuing efforts to control the illicit drug trade, and the status of the U.S. as a leading military, economic, and political power, the likelihood of the continuation of current advisory efforts and the inclusion of future military assistance advisory missions remains high.

The Republic of South Korea

In 1882, the United States concluded a treaty of peace, amity, commerce, and navigation with Korea. With the ratification of the treaty a year later, the Korean king asked the United States to send military advisors to train his army. It was five years before the United States finally dispatched three officers as its first military advisory group to Korea, The long delay and the smallness of the mission did little to sustain Korean confidence in the value of U.S. friendship.[31] This became one of the earliest foreign advisory missions in American history. It was inconsequential and failed as an effort to prevent Japanese aggression in the Far East, but it was not the final advisory effort for the U.S. in Korea. The intervening occupation of Korea by Japan, and the Cold War competition with the Communist powers forced the U.S. military to correct its earlier mistake and mount a professional and successful advisory mission for the Korean police and military. The second military advisory effort, from the end of World War II to the end of the Korean War marks the crucial period when America improved its technique for advising foreign forces. The lessons learned through successes and failures on developing another nation's security apparatus from the ground up are still included in modern advisory efforts.

At the end of WWII the Allies were startled with the rapid collapse of Japan in Manchuria and Korea. The speed with which the Soviet Union advanced through Japanese possessions in Manchuria and China worried the U.S. political and military policy makers. This forced them to rush into their plan to occupy Korea ahead of schedule with added confusion on policy development for governing the nation.[32] Starting with the post-World War II landings in Korea by the U.S. 7th Infantry Division, the forces of the southern Korean military and police

---

[31] Robert Sawyer, *Military Advisors in Korea: KMAG in War and Peace* (Washington: Office of the Chief of Military History, 1962) 4.

[32] Bryan R. Gibby, "American Advisors to the Republic of Korea: America's First Commitment in the Cold War, 1946-1950," in *Military Advising and Assistance: From Mercenaries to Privatization, 1815-2007*, Donald Stoker, ed. (New York, NY: Routledge, 2008), 81.

came under the tutelage of the U.S. military. These forces existed as a constabulary under the direct control of the U.S. from the establishment of the Korean Constabulary in January of 1946, through the establishment of the Korean Interim Government in May of 1947. U.S. forces remained in Korea after the interim government and maintained a commitment to increase Korean capability, capacity, and professionalization.[33]

Beginning in 1945, U.S. forces occupied the Korean Peninsula to the 38th Parallel in order to disarm the Japanese Army and assist in the reestablishment of local governance. Soviet forces occupied Korea North of the 38th Parallel. The physical effect of dividing the country along an unnatural boundary resulted in an imbalance. The industrial heart of the country in the north relied on the raw material and food surplus of the south, but the post-war occupation severed that link. With an unbalanced economic structure, and a nation on one hand divided physically by the Russo-American occupation agreement, and on the other divided politically by the internal factional groups, the U.S. troops began their mission in Korea. The task of establishing a viable and stable economy and enforcing internal order until Korea attained full independence promised to be a challenge demanding the highest degree of effort, skill, and tact.[34] As the American occupation of Korea replaced the forces of Japan, tremendous concern existed about the structure, size, capability, and equipping required for the new Korean military and police force. Early on in the process, the requirement for separate forces in the north and south was unknown. Furthermore, the occupying powers could make no progress on developing a security force before a governing policy and a standing government existed for the nation.[35]

Initial efforts to develop security forces for Korea failed to yield much success. U.S. efforts floundered due to economic issues in Korea, popular clamoring for political emancipation

---

[33] Young-woo Lee, "The United States and the Formation of the Republic of Korea Army 1945-1950," (Ann Arbor, Michigan: University Microfilms International, 1984), 128-129.

[34] Robert Sawyer, *Military Advisors in Korea: KMAG*, 7.

[35] Young-woo Lee, "The United States and the Formation of the Republic of Korea Army," 88.

after the Japanese occupation, differing cultural ideas on social stability, a weak South Korean Government, and a general popular desire for revolution.[36] By mid-November of 1945, the U.S. started down the road to creating a successful Korean national defense force. With remnants of Japanese supporters, elements with ties to Chinese communist forces, and Korean nationalist forces all vying for control of the populous and resources, the U.S walked a tightrope of issues to organize, train, equip and develop the forces required to maintain control south of the 38th parallel. The North Korean attack in June of 1950 caught these forces in the midst of building. The poor performance early in the war reflected this fact.[37]

Of the three cases included in this study, that of South Korea maintains the largest database of supporting literature. Complete scholarly books, journal articles, official military history, and research papers make up the bulk of the material available. The official U.S. military history on the South Korean advisory effort is Robert Sawyers' *Military Advisors in Korea: KMAG in War and Peace*. This seminal work tracks the life cycle of the Korean Military Advisory Group (KMAG) from its precursor at the end of WWII through the development of the constabulary police force, to the creation and maturity of the South Korean Military. It is a common reference widely quoted in almost every subsequent assessment of advising from the Cold War era. A second military history of the advisory effort and the statistical analysis resulting from six years of data is Dean Froehlich's two books *Military Advisors and Counterparts in Korea: an Experimental Criterion for Proficiency* and *Military Advisors and Counterparts in Korea: A Study of Personal Traits and Role Behaviors*. These works analyze and model the results of personal surveys from participants in the South Korean advisory effort in order to

---

[36] Bryan R. Gibby, "American Advisors to the Republic of Korea," 82.

[37] Robert Ramsey, *Advising Indigenous Forces: American Advisors in Korea, Vietnam, and El Salvador*. The Long War Series Occasional Paper 18 (Fort Leavenworth, KS: Combat Studies Institute Press, 2006), 5.

generalize the most effective way to train these forces. Implications arise highlighting critical aspects that are useful to military advising efforts in general.[38]

From the Korean perspective, a detailed account of the development of the modern South Korean Military and the legacy of the constabulary police force include Young-Woo Lee's dissertation "The United States and the Formation of the Republic of Korea Army 1945-1950." Lee's work is uniquely insightful because the author was an army officer in the Republic of Korea. He closes the cultural gaps found in most western works on the subject, starting his work in the mid-nineteenth century and tracing the development of the Korean army forward through forty years of Japanese occupation, into its era of western driven expansion and reorganization and finally through the crucible of war. Lee tries to explain the friction found in developing the modern Republic of Korea Army through the class in cultures and rapid modernization Korea could not avoid.[39] Nam-Sung Huh also provided a detailed view of the impacts of the political decisions and actions carried out to form the Republic of Korea Army in his 1987 dissertation "The Quest for a Bulwark of Anti-Communism: The Formation of the Republic of Korea Army Officer Corps and Its Political Socialization 1945-1950." This work sifts through the politics of a divided Korea and finds that the dynamics of the immediate post-war error led to the Korean War and frustrated the Korean people's "long dreamed hope of a unified and independent homeland."[40]

Some comprehensive histories of the era are also available. Allan Millett's two-volume history of the origins of the Korean War, *The War for Korea,* provides an analysis of the underlying cultural issues that lead to the war. The environment created by the Japanese

---

[38] Dean K. Froehlich, *Military Advisors and Counterparts in Korea: A Study of Personal Traits and Role Behaviors* (Alexandria Virginia: Human Resources Research Organization, 1971), x-xi.

[39] Young-woo Lee, "The U.S.and the Formation of the Republic of Korea Army," 6-7.

[40] Nam-sung Huh, "The Quest for a Bulwark of Anti-Communism: The Formation of the Republic of Korea Army Officer Corps and Its Political Socialization 1945-1950" (PhD Dissertation, Ohio State University, 1987), 3.

occupation shaped the way the communists Koreans, capitalists Koreans, Chinese, Russians, and Americans viewed the problem and bounded their behavior. Dr. Millett provides perspective on the key issues by viewing the interaction from the multiple perspectives of the various actors in each event. Bruce Cumings provides a comprehensive overview of the development between liberation at the end of WWII and the start of the Korean War in *The Origins of the Korean War*. He analyzes the causation of the war and provides insight and assessment that is quite different from the U.S. and South Korean perspective. He shows a sympathy for socialist governments and criticizes the early U.S. efforts to prevent the rise of a socialist dominated government in South Korea as a cause of the Korean War.

Works specific to the advisory effort in Korea include Bryan Robert Gibby's detailed analysis with "Fighting in a Korean War: the American Advisory Mission from 1946-1953." His dissertation provides an evaluation of the Korean army's capability brought about by the American military advisory missions, how these missions performed their mandated duties to organize, train, and mentor the Korean Constabulary and the Republic of Korea (ROK) Army, and how these advisors faced tremendous challenges, ranging from cultural disconnects, inexperience, scarce resources, and lack of time.[41] Alfred H. Hausrath also provided reviews of the integration of the U.S. and South Korean militaries in two separate works *The KMAG Advisor: Role and Problems of the Military Advisor in Developing an Indigenous Army for Combat Operations in Korea* and *Integration of ROK Soldiers into US Army Units (KATUSA)* with David S. Fields. The former book focuses on the modes of operation an advisor needs to overcome the culture gap between the forces as well as all the problems that arise from cross culture cooperation. The latter shows how the American experience in Korea highlights the desirability of using entire foreign military units with US organizations and utilizing of

---

[41] Bryan Gibby, "Fighting in a Korean War: The American Advisory Missions from 1946-1953" (PhD Dissertation, Ohio State University, 2004), ii.

indigenous civilian manpower as a principle of army administration as applied in theaters of operations.[42]

Not all the works available on the Korean military assistance program are in full-length books. Some of the shorter works include Robert Ramsey's study of the Korean military advisory effort "A Much Tougher Job: KMAG Combat Unit Advisors in South Korea 1950-1953." This summary of the actions of the U.S. military assistance group for Korea forms the first chapter of Ramsey's book *Advising Indigenous Forces: American Advisors in Korea, Vietnam, and El Salvador*. The work provides a concise analysis of the American effort to modernize and professionalize the South Korean Military with a view of providing a foundation for advising today. Bryan Gibby, likewise, provides a short history of the Korean assistance effort with "American Advisors to the Republic of Korea: Americas First Commitment in the Cold War 1946-1950" for the book *Military Assistance and Advising from Mercenaries to privatization 1815-2007*. In this essay he examines the ways history, language and culture complicated the effort, and shows how KMAG worked to overcome its shortfalls in organization, training, and logistics.[43]

Taken together, the volume of work on the Korea advisory effort provides detailed history, strategic context, political implications and cultural ramifications for the early actions of the military assistance programing. The initial difficulty that the South Koreans and their advisors experience early in the war receives coverage in detail. The restructuring actions that took place after the failures of 1950 get adequate attention, but as the reader comes forward in time less is information is available. The military assistance mission finally became fully successful by the summer of 1953. After that period, the amount of material available reduces significantly.

---

[42] Alfred H Hausrath and David S Fields, *Integration of ROK Soldiers into US Army Units (KATUSA)* (Bethesda, Maryland: Operational Research Office, Johns Hopkins University, 1957), 1.

[43] Bryan R. Gibby, "American Advisors to the Republic of Korea," 106.

Geography dominated the politics and culture of Korea. Although an ancient, and independent organized nation state for centuries, in the nineteenth century Korea became an unwilling pawn in the power struggle between China, Japan, and Russia for the dominant position in the Far East.[44] Located on a peninsula between China and Japan, and positioned to control the approaches to Vladivostok, Korea's geography made it a point of friction with its more powerful neighbors and subject to outside influence.[45] After the Russo-Japanese War, Japan began to exert its influence over Korea eventually wrestling it free of China's sphere of influence and absorbing it into its own. The end of Japanese control only resulted in greater disruptions in Korea's political landscape.

Politically, Korea was in a state of turmoil at the end of World War II. Like many nations that suffered Japanese occupation, Korea experience turbulence as it adjusted to the new conditions of a bi polar world.[46] After 40 years of occupation by the Japanese, the Koreans lacked an intact coherent internal government and fostered a strong dislike for the brutality of the Japanese.[47] There was bitter political infighting between communist factions, anti-communist factions, remnant Japanese influenced parties, and regional power brokers often resulted in faction on faction and mob on U.S. occupation force violence.[48] There remained tremendous debate within the various power groups whether a socialist or free market democracy should prevail. All of this occurred while it became obvious that the former allies that controlled opposing sides of the 38th parallel were transitioning into loggerheads ideological and changing the nature of global politics. Because the Japanese occupiers and Korean independence groups

---

[44] Robert Sawyer, *Military Advisors in Korea: KMAG...*, 4.

[45] Young-woo Lee, "The U.S. and the Formation of the Republic of Korea Army," 3.

[46] Bruce Cumings, *The Origin of the Korean War* (Princeton: Princeton University Press, 1990), 35-36.

[47] Young-woo Lee, "The U.S. and the Formation of the Republic of Korea Army," 4.

[48] Ibid, 80.

initially thought the Russian Soviet forces were responsible for all of Korea, the initial

government in the south formed around the Committee for the Preparation of Korean

Independence, a strongly left leaning organization.[49] When the U.S. forces arrived and the

peninsula became divided, the allies almost faced a *fait de accompli* with strongly Soviet

sympathetic elements in charge of the existing police force and various private armies patrolling

the countryside. The need for a pro-western national security and defense force capable of

handling internal duress became paramount.[50]

The failure of the initial U.S. planners to understand the subtleties of the local Korean

politics and focus on the complexity of America's role in politics on the world stage complicated

their efforts to find adequate and acceptable solutions, leading to initial difficulties within the

security forces that were developed. One political action that the U.S. took that improved their

standing in this otherwise turbulent time was to accept the notion that the Japanese enslaved the

Koreans and therefore the Koreans were not enemies of the allies. This minimized the violent

interactions between the populous and the occupation forces.[51] It was a small correct insight into

a political system that created confusion and false perceptions between the actors on both sides.

Of less utility in the long term, though assumed essential at the time, the allied decision to retain

elements of the Japanese administration in tact as a stopgap to prevent a complete leftist take-over

of the government led to friction. Due to years of occupation, Korea had few trained government

administrators. When the U.S. was unhappy with the emerging South Korean government, the

pool of qualified replacements was inadequate to meet the need to establish representative

government at all levels. At the same time, a large number of Japanese administrators existed in

South Korea who had yet to repatriate. As an interim measure, the U.S. retained the services of

---

[49] Ibid, 70.

[50] Bryan R. Gibby, "American Advisors to the Republic of Korea," 83.

[51] Young-woo Lee, "The U.S. and the Formation of the Republic of Korea Army," 66.

the Japanese administrators. Though the action provided a temporary solution, it also created enmity with the local population and a backlash that led to a rapid reduction in the program and an acceleration of training Korean personnel to function as civil administrators.[52]

Perhaps one of the greatest hurdles that the U.S. advisory effort needed to overcome was the cultural barriers between the ancient East Asian culture of Korea and the modern western culture of America that complicated the U.S. military's ability to understand Korean internal politics and acceptable behaviors. The major differences between Korean and American culture include values, beliefs, social practices, religion, history, and language. Korean culture drew much from ancient Chinese culture in the way that society was organized. The people were Confucian in ethic, believing in the supremacy of rural agricultural life and accepting an aristocratic ruling military tradition. This culture was further influenced by a long-standing policy of exclusion from the outside world to as great a degree as possible.[53] The U.S. leadership misperceived this as "archaic beliefs and superstitions," not a set of legitimate customs and beliefs.[54] This in turn led to a reinforcing of the belief that only western solutions were good, and the U.S. method was best of all. This arrogance in turn made it more difficult for early advisors to mentor their counterparts.[55] Despite the friction created by the clash of cultures, over time and under the stress of war, the advisor preparation increased enabling more success. The troubles that developed during the building of ROK security forces became apparent under the test of war, but that test changed the nature of the interaction and led to the development of a modern and professional military and police force for South Korea. As U.S. advisors began to understand that

---

[52] Robert Sawyer, *Military Advisors in Korea: KMAG,* 7-8.

[53] Ibid, 8-9

[54] Alfred H. Hausrath, *The KMAG Advisor: Role and Problems of the Military Advisor in Developing an Indigenous Army for Combat Operations in Korea* (Bethesda, Maryland: Operational Research Office, Johns Hopkins University, 1957), 22.

[55] Robert Ramsey, *Advising Indigenous Forces,* 14.

their success tied directly to the success of their counterpart, they began to find acceptance,

validity and utility in the Korean approach to resolving some issues.

Unlike the other cases included in this monograph, the U.S. was heavily involved in the

reorganization of Korean society and violated the concept of minimizing interaction with the

populous. In some ways, this was unavoidable, because a new nation came into being that had not

previously existed and therefore required a guiding hand. Hausrath's and Fields' analysis shows

that the American leaders became aware of the negative impact of their interaction with the local

population and created the Korean Augmentation Troops to the United States Army (KATUSA)

program. One of the goals of the program was to integrate selected Korean soldiers into U.S.

formations down to squad level in order to provide a Korean interface to bridge the cultural

divide and provide a local face to American operations.[56] By mid-1950, studies show that

relations between the Korean population, its soldiers, and the American forces improved

markedly over previous levels and continued to improve for the rest of the war.[57] The KATUSA

provided an additional economy of effort that reduced some interaction between Americans and

Koreans. By rotating back into South Korean Army units after service with the U.S., they

provided a means of conveying American training to the South Korean force with requiring a

commensurate advisory effort to execute the training.

From the beginning of its occupation of Korea, the U.S. was fundamentally aware that

the situation required more than just establishing a South Korean military force. The primary

advisory effort started with an authorization of 600 advisers and 600 interpreters, although it

received staffing of only 500.[58] Initial efforts focused primarily on the federal police augmented

by a Korean Constabulary and then expanded to include a Korean Army after the establishment

---

[56] Hausrath and Fields, *Integration of ROK Soldiers*, 11.

[57] Ibid, 37.

[58] Robert Ramsey, *Advising Indigenous Forces*, 10.

of South Korean Interim Government in 1947.[59] The constabulary proved adequate at reducing the level of political violence that arose with the initiation of South Korean state only after it underwent internal purges reducing the number of socialist and communist party sympathizers in its ranks. Even after its reformation, it proved inadequate at overcoming existential threats against the state.[60] In the first two years of the Korean War, the U.S. had to commit forces to conduct counter-guerrilla operation, but by late 1951 the South Korean police and army forces proved capable of conducting the preponderance of the counter-guerrilla operations as evidenced in Operation RATKILLER and other.[61] The South Korean Army also underwent a period of failure early in the war culminating with the May 1951 inactivation and dissolution of III ROK Corps. However, these failings brought on renewed and far more intense training for the South Korean Army as well as expansion in its capability and strength. By 1952, a reversal of the negative trend occurred, and by 1953, the Republic of Korea's Army proved capable of successful sustained operations.[62]

Prior to the Korean War, assignment as an adviser was a year unaccompanied or two years if the advisor brought his family.[63] Selection for advising duty was not career enhancing, and the selection process was not rigorous. The duty received poor recognition as to its importance and U.S. personnel preferred to serve in U.S. This situation resulted in the advisory effort being constantly understrength. Once the Korean War started, the personnel assignment policy for advisers accidentally improved the capacity of the program. Because of the chronic shortage in advisers, the points required to rotate out of the job increased. While a U.S. combat soldier needed 38 points to rotate out of his assignment, he earned 4 points per month. An advisor

---

[59] Bryan R. Gibby, "American Advisors to the Republic of Korea," 82.

[60] Birtle, *U.S. Army Counterinsurgency 1942-1976*, 88.

[61] Ibid, 102.

[62] Robert Ramsey, *Advising Indigenous Forces*, 8.

[63] Ibid, 12.

required 40 points to rotate and only earned 3 points per month.[64] In part because Advisors to the Korean constabulary and military started the job deficient on training in the Korean culture or methods of engaging their Korean counterparts, the additional two months provided time to gain an improved understanding of the environment, increasing the strength of the partnership between adviser and his Korean partner. Overall, it required between 6 and 8 years to organize, train equip and professionalize the South Korean security forces to the level that they could conduct internal and external security at sufficient levels.

Initially, the Americans prepared their advisors poorly for success. Military personnel did not view advisor duty as desirable, and the service made no effort to ensure qualified quality personnel received selection for the duty, despite the fact that advisors mentored Korean counterparts who outranked them by two to three ranks.[65] Language training was not required, and efforts to train advisors to speak Hangul largely died from lack of interest.[66] The advisory effort overcame this problem overcome through hiring Korean university students with English language skills to act as interpreters. While not a perfect solution, it proved adequate. As the program developed, the leadership also instituted required training in culture and the techniques of advising culminating in the 1953 Eighth U.S. Army's KMAG Handbook. The handbook not only taught advisors the essentials of living, working and fighting with Koreans, but also, most importantly, how to point out and critique a counterpart's mistakes without causing him to culturally loose face.[67] Understanding the problem through the lens of the Korean who would remain to deal with the ramifications of any imposed solutions created positive traction for moving forward with a successful program

---

[64] Ibid, 12.

[65] Ibid, 11.

[66] Ibid, 15.

[67] Eighth U.S. Army, *KMAG Handbook* (Eighth Army Publishing Directorate, 1953), 22.

El Salvador

El Salvador has a long history of conflict between its indigenous native peoples and European settlers from the colonial era. This conflict between the natives and Europeans also reflected the struggle between the poor, disposed working class and the wealthy land owning class. The government suffered from an inability to control the population and failed to provide for the needs of the poor. When Nicaragua fell under the dominance of a Marxist revolution, the military of El Salvador foresaw that ineffective government could lead to a similar fall in their own state and therefore staged a coup to establish a unified centralist government. The Salvadorian military stated that the basis for the 15 October 1979 coup was the perception of election fraud that prevented the military's preferred candidate from winning.[68] The junta promised many reforms but failed to bring about promises, resulting in multiple socialist and communist guerrilla groups rising up in resistance to the central government. When the five major rebel groups merge in 1980, they began to overwhelm the Salvadorian security forces. The leftist government of Nicaragua supported the insurgency and the government of El Salvador could not stand up to this threat without external assistance. The United States felt compelled to respond to prevent a communist takeover and acted with three policy goals: combat, deter, or defeat the insurgency; strengthen Salvadorian democratic principles, institutions, and structure; and achieve broad-based socioeconomic development.[69] For 12 years, the U.S. struggled to contain the situation in El Salvador, torn between stopping communist expansion and reforming a repressive government. The primary challenge the U.S. faced was the dual task of assisting with the largest military build-up in Central American history while training the Salvadorian force to

---

[68] Kimbra L. Fishel and Edwin G. Corr, "UN Peace Operations in El Salvador: The Manwaring Paradigm in a Traditional Setting," in *The Savage Wars of Peace: Towards a New Paradigm of Peace Operations,* John T. Fishel, ed. (Boulder, CO: Westview Press, 1998), 42.

[69] Michael Childress, *The Effectiveness of U.S. Training Efforts in Internal Defense and Development: The Case of El Salvador and Honduras* (Santa Monica, CA: Rand, 1995), 18.

be militarily effective and politically inactive.[70] A unique and critical factor in the case of El Salvador was the political decision in the United States to cap the advisor manpower at 55, not only was it small in comparison to the other cases, but its desired outcome was limited in scope as well.[71]

The literature concerning the Salvadorian advisory effort is not as complete as that of South Korea. Michael Hennelly's essay "U.S. Policy in El Salvador: Creating Beauty or the Beast," provides an analysis of the policy decisions made concerning El Salvador and the "capability of the United States to foster democratic development and American concepts of military professionalism elsewhere."[72] Chapter three of Robert D. Ramsey's *Advising Indigenous Forces: American Advisors in Korea, Vietnam, and El Salvador* provides a concise history of the effort in El Salvador, clearly defining the structure, roles, selection, and training of the advisors, as well as investigating the social and cultural implications of the operation. Ramsey highlights the U.S. political attempts to keep the mission simple, sustainable, small, and Salvadorian.[73] Ramsey's, *Advise for Advisors*, includes an official after action report from the U.S. operations, plans and training team for the Salvadorian Second Military Zone for 1991 and 1992. These findings also include 36 lessons learned by the advisors on how to improve future efforts. Kimbra Fishel and Edwin Corr provide a short study of the legitimacy the U.S. effort provided in moving both the FMLN and the Salvadorian government to a negotiated settlement in their essay "UN Peace Operations in El Salvador: The Manwaring Paradigm in a Traditional Setting" from the book *The Savage Wars of Peace: Towards a New Paradigm of Peace Operations*. While the work focuses on peacekeeping in the 1990s, it evaluates the grievances that started the conflict and the

---

[70] Michael J. Hennelly, "U.S. Policy in El Salvador: Creating Beauty or the Beast," *Parameters*, (Spring 1993), 59-60.

[71] Ramsey, *Advising Indigenous Forces*, 83.

[72] Hennelly, "U.S. Policy in El Salvador," 60.

[73] Ramsey, *Advising Indigenous Forces*, 85.

mechanisms that brought about its end. American efforts to professionalize the Salvadorian security forces and increase democratic reform set the conditions for the peaceful resolution, but the economic, political, and military influence the U.S. exerted on both sides made a negotiated settlement possible.[74] Michael Childress' RAND study *The Effectiveness of U.S. Training Efforts in Internal Defense and Development* tracks the $4.5 billion spent by the U.S. to transform the society of El Salvador and the "mixed success of U.S. training."[75]

As well as analytical works, first-hand accounts of the Salvadorian advisory mission are also available. Victor Rosello's "Lessons from El Salvador" provide a concise series of observations from his time as an advisor to the Salvadorian security forces. Cecil Bailey's "OPATT: The U.S. Army SF Advisers in El Salvador" providers a much more critical view, highlighting some of the issues in the twelve year program that almost caused it to fail from the lens of his two tours as an advisor in El Salvador. Where Rosello shows El Salvador as a shining example of U.S. commitment in the region,[76] Bailey faults the U.S. presence for never being clearly defined, far too under-resourced, and subject to stonewalling by a host government that did not want to reform itself in exchange for U.S. assistance.[77]

The root cause of the insurgency and a critical issue behind the U.S. counterinsurgency efforts revolved around economic opportunity. The social and political stratification of society in El Salvador made the majority of the population sympathetic towards the insurgency. During the 1970s, it became clear that the Salvadoran government was incapable of managing internal pressures for political and economic change.[78] The government forces not only engaged in

---

[74] Fishel and Corr, "UN Peace Operations in El Salvador," 49-50.

[75] Childress, *Effectiveness of U.S. Training Efforts*, 27.

[76] Victor M. Rosello, "Lessons from El Salvador," *Parameters* (Winter 1993-1994), 108.

[77] Cecil E. Bailey, "OPATT: The U.S. Army Advisers in El Salvador," *Special Warfare* (December 2004), 27.

[78] Hennelly, "U.S. Policy in El Salvador," 61.

political oppression, but, more menacingly, the Salvadorian military had links to death squads. The military and death squads combined were responsible for 10,000 politically motivated killings in1981.[79] Even the junta president Jose Napoleon Duarte acknowledged that the guerrillas might have had good reasons for taking up arms without hope for "economic reform, social justice, or free elections while under the tyranny of oligarchy aligned with armed forces."[80] The U.S. congress saw this as a twofold problem, first, that the military had to be reformed, and second, that the economic situation required improvement. Additionally congress believed that a liberalized military could assist with economic development, that it could be trained to operate with "nation- building" skills for its own country.[81]

Culturally, El Salvador was similar to many Latin American countries with a Spanish past. Over time, however, it developed its own unique society based on its own development challenges and the responses taken towards them. As a country of relatively small geographic size, it had experienced population pressures and land distribution issues that led to the insurgency.[82] In 1969, overpopulation led to a migration and border delineation issue with neighboring Honduras. The problem escalated until summer, when dispute in a series of international sporting matches triggered the 100-hour long "Football War."[83] The countryside had a history of peasant uprisings and brutal repressions, including the 1931 *Mantanza* or genocide of the indigenous people in the western districts by the government.[84] Social systems reinforced the importance of personal friendships and family ties resulting in rampant nepotism and a hesitancy

---

[79] Childress, *Effectiveness of U.S. Training Efforts*, 19.

[80] Fischel and Corr, "UN Peace Operations in El Salvador," 43.

[81] Childress, *Effectiveness of U.S. Training Efforts*, 11.

[82] Ramsey, *Advising Indigenous Forces*, 92.

[83] Thomas P. Anderson, *The War of the Dispossessed: Honduras and El Salvador 1969* (Lincoln, NE: University of Nebraska Press, 1981), 73-74.

[84] Ramsey, *Advising Indigenous Forces*, 92.

to be confrontational. These two factors together created a tradition of corruption for Salvadorians that most U.S. observers found deplorable.[85]

The only cultural factors that played to U.S. strengths were the Spanish language and the general region. The American Army had more than an adequate supply of Special Forces personnel who were Spanish speakers and familiar with the Central American region if not El Salvador in particular. Frequent interaction with many countries in the region gave the American military and policymakers familiarity with the regional issues, and a perceived understanding of the underlying issues surrounding the insurgency. While almost a century of U.S. involvement in Latin America exposed some negative feelings towards perceived American Imperialism in the region, elements of cultural understanding existed for both the U.S. advisors and their Salvadoran counterparts. In addition, the Salvadoran junta knew that the U.S. viewed Central America as its primary security interest and would aid in efforts to prevent the rise of another leftist government in the region.[86]

Coming less than a decade after Vietnam, the American military and political authority wanted above all to avoid a repeat of that experience. Prior to the FMLN offensive in 1981, the American effort consisted of sending a handful of observers on a fact-finding mission. Once Ronald Reagan became president, however, official policy towards El Salvador changed due to the perception of a resurgent Soviet threat to the western hemisphere based on massive modernization of the Soviet military, the continuing issue of a communist Cuba, and the rise of the Sandinista government in Nicaragua.[87] This change in viewpoint led the political leadership in the U.S. to walk a tightrope between preventing the fall of a pro-western government, and keeping the U.S. commitment minimal. The politicians evaluated the Salvadorian issue to be of

---

[85] Ibid, 93-94.

[86] Fischel and Corr, "UN Peace Operations in El Salvador," 49.

[87] Hennelly, "U.S. Policy in El Salvador," 60-61.

minor importance in the grand scheme of confronting the soviets worldwide, and also assumed the American people had little stomach for another large counterinsurgency so soon after Vietnam.[88] The engagement strategy that developed in result to the political situation was one of limited, targeted foreign internal defense and development.

The El Salvador experience generally validated the US Army's post-Vietnam Foreign Internal Defense doctrine in countering insurgency: El Salvador demonstrated the merits of relegating US involvement to a strictly supporting role and pushing to reform the societal issues behind the problem concurrent with reforming and training the host country military.[89] This policy reflects the funding steam of the whole El Salvador counterinsurgency effort. Over 12 years of the program, $1 billion went to military aid, including foreign military sales,[90] while $3.5 billion went to economic assistance and internal development, most administered through the U.S. State Department's Agency for International Development (AID).[91] When contemplating the funding for this operation, Congress felt compelled to limit the size of the military component of the assistance effort to 55 personnel inside El Salvador and limit them to strict non-combat missions.[92] Clearly, the focus was on more than a military solution to the problem.

The decision to minimize the military footprint hampered the advisory effort's ability to expand to forces beyond the El Salvadorian armed forces (ESAF). Additionally, the Salvadorian National Police found themselves politically subjugated to the military and acting as an adjunct military force.[93] As it turned out, the military dominated not only the police, but also the

---

[88] Bailey, "OPATT," 18.

[89] Rosello, "Lessons from El Salvador," 102.

[90] Childress, *Effectiveness of U.S. Training Efforts*, 21.

[91] Ibid, 26.

[92] Rosello, "Lessons from El Salvador," 103.

[93] Hennelly, "U.S. Policy in El Salvador," 62.

judiciary.[94] Finally, the U.S. training teams consisted almost exclusively of infantry, special forces, and intelligence teams with a single team built around military police capacity.[95] Eventually the National Police disbanded and the National Civil Police formed as a condition before the FMLF would come to terms for a negotiated settlement.[96]

Despite this small advisor footprint inside El Salvador, the Operations Plans and Assistance Training Team (OPATT) managed the growth of Salvadoran defense forces from 11,000 to 56,000 in six years.[97] At the same time this growth in forces occurred, the Americans implemented a round of human rights and "constabulary force training" in conjunction with a depoliticization of the military campaign to change the social culture prevalent inside the ESAF.[98] The U.S. military was able to increase training throughput by sending Salvadorian soldiers to Honduras and the U.S. to train. Training in the U.S. included the School of the Americas as well as separate training for whole units up to battalion size. This out of country training eased the load on the OPATT.

While unit tactical training was successful, OPATT saw the critical component of its overall training plan as the professionalization of the force. The result of the professionalism training was a split in the officer corps between a generation that underwent U.S. training and those that did not. Those new units that received training in humane behavior and human rights proved far less likely to commit atrocities and overall reduced tensions between the populous and the government, allowing a negotiated result.[99] Established units however proved far more

---

[94] Childress, *Effectiveness of U.S. Training Efforts*, 40.

[95] Ramsey, *Advising Indigenous Forces*, 88.

[96] Fischel and Corr, "UN Peace Operations in El Salvador," 52.

[97] Ibid,86.

[98] Childress, *Effectiveness of U.S. Training Efforts*, 20 and 23.

[99] Ibid, 39.

difficult to retrain, and less likely to accept the U.S. methods whole-heartedly.[100] The FMLN expressed during the peace negotiations that success at reforming the government-controlled security was one of the principle reasons the negotiations were possible at all.[101]

The policy decision to minimize the U.S. presence in El Salvador created the positive impact of putting a Salvadorian face on the counterinsurgency from the beginning and a complicating factor by limiting the trainers available for the work of military assistance advising. This low ratio of troops to task created a useful benefit. As the OPATT element inside El Salvador remained small, the available pool of Spanish speaking trained advisors and trainers was substantial.[102] Many of the OPATT leadership had previous advising experience in Vietnam or elsewhere in Latin America, and several advisors rotated through multiple assignments to the OPATT.[103] Other U.S. soldiers received only three days of general advisor training not specific to El Salvador.[104] The advisors themselves found that it required three to six months to get accustomed to their area of operations and the unit they supported. As the typical assignment was a one year unaccompanied tour, this translated to advisors that achieved peak efficiency for only about half of their tour. Ambassador Pickering complained that the Army's rotational system to trade out advisors resulted in "constantly relearning old lessons."[105] The training facility in Honduras received its trainers from 7th Special Forces Group on a rotational basis for 90-180 day assignments.[106] The turnover negatively affected the trainers' abilities to understand the units they

---

[100] Ramsey, *Advising Indigenous Forces*, 99.

[101] Childress, *Effectiveness of U.S. Training Efforts*, 38.

[102] Ramsey, *Advising Indigenous Forces*, 92.

[103] Waghelstein, "Ruminations of a Wooly Mammoth," 165.

[104] Ramsey, *Advising Indigenous Forces*, 91.

[105] Ibid, 90.

[106] Waghelstein, "Ruminations of a Wooly Mammoth," 164.

were responsible for developing. The resulting slow degree of progress resulted in the mission taking 12 years to complete.

The foreign internal defense mission for El Salvador provided several useful insights for developing a successful model for future military assistance advising. Both positive and negative results arise from the experience, highlighting actions that result in success. The first area of consideration is the importance of local culture and politics. While the decision to provide military assistance is a U.S. policy decision, local social and political conditions limit the degree of effectiveness of the program. In the case of El Salvador, the understanding of the economic disenfranchisement of large segments of the population and the high level of political power wielded by the ESAF led to a program designed to counter these issues. Though it took 12 years, the gradual improvement in both areas provided a basis to achieving the negotiated solution the U.S. sought. The second critical factor is the decision to keep a local face on the mission. This factor gives legitimacy to the mission in the eyes of the locals that an alien U.S. presence as the lead cannot match. Furthermore, the actions of key local officials involved in approving and guiding the training effort creates greater momentum for buy in by the forces receiving training. The third area of utility for the model focuses on other security forces. When the assistance effort balances to account for nonmilitary security agencies as well as the military, the transition occurs faster and to a greater degree than when it includes the military alone. In El Salvador, the militarization of the police force and over politicization of the ESAF significantly complicated this issue. Ultimately, the National Police disbanded entirely to create a force capable of serving the populous fairly and justly. The fourth area for consideration is that of cultural exposure on the advisor. The time required to familiarize a new advisor to the environment is time spent at less than optimal capability. In El Salvador, the 90-180 day rotation of schoolhouse trainers and the one-year rotation of advisors translated into a force that progressed in its development slowly. Some of this was overcome by the large pool of Latin American focused trainers provided by 7th

Special Forces Group, but that advantage may not exist in future efforts. A more rapid rate of professionalization is achievable if trainers remain as trainers for longer periods.

Colombia

Colombia became a partner for a U.S. military assistance effort initially in response to an insurgency developing under Cuban influence. The Marxist insurgency started in the 1960s, though the threat to the Colombian government transitioned in a matter of 40 years into a complex environment involving international drug cartels, paramilitary organizations, and the original fractured insurgencies coalesced into a major threat to the sovereignty of the state. Though the problems for Colombia started as an insurgency in the 1960s, within 20 years the drug cartels became a greater source of disruption for Colombian autonomy. As a case, Colombia provides a unique perspective because the purpose of its advisory effort changed over time. U.S. involvement in Colombia traces back to the Theodore Roosevelt error of gunboat diplomacy and the creation of Panama as an independent state.[107] For most of the twentieth century, the U.S. invested far more effort into developing Panama than Colombia. When Colombia opted to assisting the U.N. operations in Korea, it sent a battalion of 1000 soldiers assigned to the U.S. 21st Infantry Regiment, 24th Infantry Division. These forces, trained in the American methods of conducting operations, returned from Korea and infused a sense of professionalism into the Colombian Army.[108]

The rise of a communist insurgency eventually drove the U.S. to action in Colombia. The initial U.S. MILGROUP sent to assist in modernizing Colombia's military consisted of as few as six personnel.[109] The Colombian conflict, which started with the launch of a communist insurgency, officially is a three-sided conflict among the communist guerillas, the government

---

[107] Max Boot, *The Savage Wars of Peace: Small Wars and the Rise of American Power* (New York, NY: Basic Books, 2002), 134.

[108] Douglas Porch and Christopher W. Muller, "Imperial Grunts Revisited: The U.S. Advisory Mission in Colombia," in *Military Advising and Assistance: From Mercenaries to Privatization, 1815-2007*, Donald Stoker, ed. (New York, NY: Routledge, 2008), 170.

[109] Ibid, 171.

and right-wing paramilitary groups.[110] The U.S. advisor effort expanded over time from a simple effort to shore Colombia up against a Communist based insurgency, through a period of primarily counter-narcotics enforcement training, to a hybrid of counterinsurgency, counter-narcotics, and elimination of terrorist organizations.

The assassination of Colombian presidential hopeful Luis Carlos Galán by the Medellín drug cartel in August 1989 led Colombian president Virgilio Barco to impose emergency security measures on the country, and the U.S. to announce that it might consider the deployment of military forces to assist Colombia in the war on drugs.[111] On September 15, 1989, President George Herbert Walker Bush announced that military and law enforcement assistance would increase to help the Andean nations of Colombia, Bolivia, and Peru combat illicit drug producers and traffickers. By mid-September, there were 50-100 US military advisers in Colombia in connection with the transport and training in the use of U.S. military equipment, plus seven Special Forces teams of 2-12 persons to train troops in the three countries.[112] These military assistance missions formed from a series of operations authorized by President George H. W. Bush and congress collectively known as the Andean Initiative.

The 1990 Andean Initiative provided Colombia with a $200 million aid package intended to combat drugs, but comprised largely of resources to train and equip the Colombian military.[113] After a change in government in Bogata to one less friendly to the U.S., aid and the advisory

---

[110] Oeindrila Dubey and Suresh Naiduz, *Bases, Bullets and Ballots: the Effect of U.S. Military Aid on Political Conflict in Colombia*, Working Paper 197 (Washington D.C.: Center for Global Development, January 2010), 6.

[111] Ethan Bronner, "US aide talks of troop help for Colombia," *The Baltimore Sun*, August 21, 1989, 1.

[112] Richard F. Grimmett, "Instances of Use of United States Armed Forces Abroad, 1798 – 2004" Congressional Research Service report RL30172 (Washington D.C.: Congressional Research Service, October 2004), http://www.au.af.mil/au/awc/awcgate/crs/rl30172 htm (Accessed August 12, 2011).

[113] Adam Isacson, "The U.S. military in the war on drugs," in C. Youngers and E. Rosin, ed, *Drugs and Democracy in Latin America: The Impact of US Policy* (Boulder, Colorado: Lynne Rienner Publishers, 2005), 17.

effort stalled, falling sharply only to resurge under a more pro-U.S. government. In 2000, "Plan Colombia" developed initially as 1.2 billion dollars of aid targeted to train and equip the Colombian military and police for counter-narcotics operations. While Plan Colombia appeared as a new program, it actually continued previous U.S. policy and involvement in Colombia. The start of the Global War on Terror allowed for the application of additional funds and training resources against the situation and additionally expanded the U.S. mission in Colombia to include counter-terrorism as well as counter-drug and counter-insurgency training. This expansion of support was highly militarized with over 80 percent going to the military and police.[114]

The current Colombian Civil War represents a continuation of the four decades old conflict between left-wing guerillas, the state, and right-wing paramilitary groups, which collude with the government military in countering the guerillas. The current-day insurgency is led by the Armed Revolutionary Forces of Colombia (FARC by its Spanish acronym), whose strength is roughly 16,000-20,000 combatants, and the National Liberation Army (ELN), which is estimated to have 4,000-6,000 fighters.[115] In 1997, the disparate paramilitary groups formed an umbrella organization called the United Self-Defense Forces of Colombia (AUC), which had roughly 30,000 fighters at its peak strength.[116] The complexity of the war draws amplification from the narco-terrorist organization and drug cartels that use the disruption of state control as a means to create space to conduct their own activities.[117]

The case of the advisory effort in Colombia is least written about of the three in this analysis. One of the glaring issues is the lack of solid first-hand accounts of operations in Colombia in full-length book format. While some chapter length articles in compilation books

---

[114] Porch and Muller, "Imperial Guns Revisited," 172.

[115] Dubey and Naiduz, *Bases, Bullets and Ballots*, 6.

[116] Ibid, 6.

[117] Michael Evans, "War in Columbia Volume III: Conditioning Security Assistance," National Security Archive Electronic Briefing Book No. 69, http://www.gwu.edu/~nsarchiv/NSAEBB/NSAEBB69/part3 html (accessed August 7, 2011).

exist, and a few more than two dozen position papers and scholarly research documents exist that at least partially cover the advisory effort, none have the comprehensive detail that are available in books that cover the other three case. Max Boot's *The Savage Wars of Peace* provides a concise history of Panama's separation from Colombia in the early twentieth century and the ramifications this display of American gunboat diplomacy had on the region, both positive and negative including the "Caribbean Constabulary" the U.S. developed and maintained to keep the peace in the region afterwards.

Dennis M. Rempe provides a scholarly research of Columbia in the 50s and 60s and the long-term impacts that the violent period known as *La Violencia* has on the problems the country faces today. His assessment of the culture and security found in *The Past as Prologue: A History of Counterinsurgency Policy in Colombia, 1958-66* is useful. Additionally, his primary finding that "security of the state does not necessary reflect security for its citizens" finds basis in 50 years of violence as political discourse.[118] He shows that when the state acts against its own citizens with unchecked violence it generates the conditions that allow insurgencies to grow.

Bob Graham, Brent Scowcroft, and Michael Shifter collaborated on "Toward Greater Peace and Security in Colombia, Forging a Constructive U.S. Policy" in order to examine the origins of the insurgency in Columbia and map out a way ahead for U.S. policy. They recommend a global approach based on deepening democracy, protecting human rights, expanding economic partnership, and fighting drugs.[119] "Imperial Grunts Revisited: The U.S. Advisory Mission in Colombia," by Douglas Porch and Christopher W. Muller provided the most useful direct analysis of the advisory effort in Colombia. The work analyzed the similarities

---

[118] Dennis M. Rempe, *The Past as Prologue: A History of Counterinsurgency Policy in Colombia, 1958-66* (Carlisle, PA: Strategic Studies Institute, U.S. Army War College, 2002), 39.

[119] Bob Graham, Brent Scowcroft and Michael Shifter, "Toward Greater Peace and Security in Colombia, Forging a Constructive U.S. Policy" (Washington D.C.: Council on Foreign Relations 2000), viii.

between the advisory mission in El Salvador and that of Colombia. It points out that the natural outcome of the reforms in military and police lead to substantial increases in efficient professionalize forces, expanding security in the country, but that the reforms need to lead to political reforms in order to provide long lasting stability.[120]

Michael Evan's three part online summary "War in Colombia" proved very useful due to its direct links to source documents, and news articles covering the expansion of the advisory effort between 1988 and 2002. The article expressed a bias against the advisory effort, however, and states the U.S.-supported counterdrug programs are not only ineffective, but also increasingly dangerous to the population in Colombia, based on human rights abuses from the same military and police forces the Americans trained.[121] Oeindrila Dubey and Suresh Naiduz provide a more detailed and balanced review of the same U.S. aid and efforts at advising Colombian forces in their paper analyzing the micro level data on democracy and violence between 1988 and 2005. *Bases, Bullets and Ballots: the Effect of U.S. Military Aid on Political Conflict in Colombia* shows that U.S. efforts to professionalize the Colombian military and police forces have been marginally effective, the side effect has been much more capable and violent paramilitary factions.[122]

Adam Isacson examines the results of the advisory effort and military aid to Colombia in his chapter "The U.S. military in the War on Drugs" from *Drugs and Democracy in Latin America: The Impact of US Policy*. He finds that the mission has mixed results and may be far from the most efficient method to solve the crisis. In *Colombia's Resurrection: Alternative Development is the Key to Democratic Security*, Adam Lum Fleming analyzes the way

---

[120] Porch and Muller, "Imperial Guns Revisited," 187.

[121] Michael Evans, "War in Columbia Volume I: The Andean Strategy", National Security Archive Electronic Briefing Book No. 69, http://www.gwu.edu/~nsarchiv/NSAEBB/NSAEBB69/part1 html (accessed August 7, 2011).

[122] Dubey and Naiduz, *Bases, Bullets and Ballots*, 3.

development as well as security force training must both be advanced to provide a strategy to overcoming the insurgency. [123]

In addition to scholarly research and case study analysis, several general news articles provided detailed insight into specific aspects of the Columbian situation that proved useful. Colonel William Mendel's article "Colombia's Threats to Regional Security" provides a more positive analysis for the future of Colombia if the government hardens its stance against the narco-guerrillas, increasing the combat correlations inside Colombia in ways that dramatically favor the Colombian army. He postulates that with such action by the military disaffection would dissipate, and real support for a combined anti-outlaw plan from Colombia's neighbors could develop.[124] Ethan Bronner provides the historic rationale for expanding the U.S. mission in "US Aide Talks of Troop Help for Colombia." Dr. Thomas A Marks (Ph.D.) provides relevant analysis and lessons learned from the counterinsurgency fight in Colombia with "A Model for Counterinsurgency: Uribe's Colombia (2002-2006) vs FARC".

Politics and culture play significant impacts in the way that the Colombian insurgency started, spread, and the manner in which the state attempts to fight it. First, geography shapes the culture of Colombia. Colombia is a large nation, the size of Texas, Oklahoma, and New Mexico combined. The towering, snowcapped Andes Mountains bisect Colombia from north to south, and a dense jungle in the south competes with the Amazon's rain forest. Rivers crisscross southern Colombia and swamps make movement of military units difficult or next to impossible. Because the state cannot control its own territory, the economy suffers and there is a disparity of wealth between the cities and the countryside.[125] This vast and segmented terrain creates

---

[123] Adam Lum Fleming, *Colombia's Resurrection: Alternative Development is the Key to Democratic Security* (Monterey, CA: Naval Postgraduate School, 2004), 16.

[124] William W. Mendel, "Colombia's Threats to Regional Security," *Military Review* (May-June 2001), 13.

[125] Alfred A. Valenzuela and Victor M. Rosello, "Expanding Roles and Missions in the War on Drugs and Terrorism: El Salvador and Colombia," *Military Review* (March- April 2004), 31.

difficulties for the central state to control the entire state. The very weakness of the state enables substantial capture and diversion of given resources, or the establishments of zones controlled by dissident groups.[126] Colombia's size and immense geostrategic importance, located astride two oceans, and its strong economy, with viable and growing north-south trade route, make it crucial to the United States and the rest of the world community. Historically, many of Colombia's remote regions have interacted more easily with trade centers outside Colombia, finding the lines of drift into other countries more useful than the cross-compartment routes within their own.[127][128]

Despite the boundaries to governmental control, Colombia maintains a tradition of democracy and civilian control of the military. Colombia was the first constitutional government of South America, established in 1811. It is the only South American country that has never had a coup. The Liberal and Conservative parties, founded in 1848 and 1849 respectively, are two of the oldest surviving political parties in the Americas.[129] These two sets of oligarchic power brokers influence Colombia's version of democracy, resulting in the current extremely troubling turmoil. Political brinksmanship between the two parties occasionally erupts into violence, most notably in the Thousand Days War (1899–1902) and *La Violencia*, beginning in 1948.[130] A generation of Colombians grew up thinking violence was a normal way of life. Unable to find employment and feeling disenfranchised by the government, many turned to banditry and some to revolution and class-oriented goals.[131] Since the 1960s, government forces, left-wing insurgents

---

[126] Dubey and Naiduz, *Bases, Bullets and Ballots*, 3-4.

[127] Mendel, "Colombia's Threats," 14.

[128] This is consistent with Jefferey Herbst's international relations theories and his model for a state's attempts to consolidate power found in his book *States and Power in Africa: Comparative Lessons in Authority and Control* (Princeton: Princeton University Press, 2000).

[129] Rempe, *The Past as Prologue*, 2

[130] Ibid, 3.

[131] Michael Shifter, "Colombia at War," *Current History* vol 98 (March 1999), 116-117.

and right-wing paramilitaries have been engaged in the continent's longest-running armed conflict.

The U.S. entered this complex political situation knowing the difficulties involved. The political authority in Washington understood that Colombia's core, underlying problem is one of state authority and the maintenance of public order. The critical problem is the capacity to govern, to perform key functions. Other problems, including human rights violations and drug production and trafficking, are manifestations of the authority crisis, and in turn exacerbate the conflict.[132] From the early engagement of the 1960s through the current expanded mission, the history of U.S. intervention against Colombia in the early 20th century created a subcontext of imperial aggression that required careful public relations management. In some cases, drug organizations attempted to use the Colombian government's reliance on U.S. assistance as an indicator that it lacked legitimacy.[133] Over the course of the 40-year insurgency, the advisory expanded from a small military only focus to a larger police and military effort as the drug war escalated and overtook the insurgency as the high profile problem. After the terror attacks of September 11, 2001, the political environment changed again allowing the U.S. to put in place an even larger effort aimed at the full spectrum of the threat but umbrella under the counter-terrorism banner.[134]

In its earliest format, the U.S. Advisory effort was as small as possible. Initially consisting of six personnel providing efforts to professionalize the Colombian Army, the force available for the advisory mission expanded as the Colombian military and the perceived threat to the U.S. from Colombia's failure grew.[135] As in El Salvador, one way advisory forces remained

---

[132] Graham, Scowcroft, and Shifter, "Toward Greater Peace," 11.

[133] Porch and Muller, "Imperial Guns Revisited," 177-178.

[134] Ibid, 172.

[135] Michael Evans, "War in Columbia Volume I," http://www.gwu.edu/~nsarchiv/NSAEBB/ NSAEBB69/part1 html (accessed August 7, 2011).

small, was by sending Colombian soldiers to schooling in the United States, or regional schools in Panama and Honduras.[136] After the Andean Strategy began in 1989 then Plan Colombia came into being a year later, the U.S. Congress began to authorize greater spending on assistance to Colombia. After the Global War on Terror began, even more funding, equipment and personnel became available. This increase in capacity and capability came at the cost of militarizing a program that prior to this maintained a heavy dose of civil-political primacy.[137] The U.S. forces available doubled between 2001 and 2006 to 800 military personnel backed up by 600 civilian security sector contractors.[138] The GWOT aid package aimed at training and equipping the Colombian military for counter-narcotics operations, rather than pursuing counter-insurgency. However, given the guerillas involvement in the drug trade, the line between these two objectives has remained blurry, and it is impossible to distinguish the counter-narcotics and counterinsurgency components of U.S. aid.[139]

Another way the U.S. minimized the military manpower required for advisory forces prior to 2001 was the use of nonmilitary agencies to conduct military assistance. Agencies such as the U.S. Justice Department, the Drug Enforcement Agency, Federal Bureau of Investigations, and United States Agency for International Development provided the resourcing and support toward this program. The effort assisted military and police agencies chiefly aimed at counter-narcotics, but including support for alternative development, judicial reform, and rule of law training.[140] Over the past two decades, the United States has provided nearly $5 billion in military

---

[136] Porch and Muller, "Imperial Guns Revisited," 171.

[137] Michael Evans, "War in Columbia Volume ," http://www.gwu.edu/~nsarchiv/NSAEBB/ NSAEBB69/part1 html (accessed August 7, 2011).

[138] Porch and Muller, "Imperial Guns Revisited," 172.

[139] Dubey and Naiduz, *Bases, Bullets and Ballots*, 7.

[140] Graham, Scowcroft, and Shifter, "Toward Greater Peace," 18.

aid, with the stated aim of supporting counter-narcotics and counter-insurgency efforts, however, up to 80% of U.S. aid to Columbia funnels into military and police programs annually.[141]

From the beginning of the assistance effort to Colombia, the concept that this was a long-term mission for the U.S. permeated the operation. The U.S. Military Group –Colombia (MILGP-COL) organized with two year, permanent duty billets augmented with three and six month temporary duty personnel. While the organizational staff tends to be permanent duty billets, temporary duty soldiers accomplish much of the actual training. Contractors who perform administrative and logistics functions in turn support this force.[142] These civilians often possess detailed understanding of the Colombian culture, having served there previously in a military capacity. Despite over forty years of experience with training Colombia's military and police forces and an established system for retaining subject matter experts in the MILGP, the Colombian leadership still complains that the US training forces experience too significant a turnover in personnel.[143]

Analysis of the case study from Colombia reveals that focused effort over the long-term leads to training solutions that fit within the difficult framework of regional politics. While this advisory effort is still on going, improvements continue to become observable in Colombia. Since 2002, homicides have fallen by 30 percent, massacres (the killing of three or more persons at one time) by 61 percent, kidnappings by 51 percent, and acts of terrorism by 56 percent. If public safety is a measure of well-being, most Colombians are better off today.[144] Even the few negative aspects of the operation received oversight from the U.S. Congress. When paramilitary violence trended upward in areas under Colombian military control, the link to the military's tacit support

---

[141] Dubey and Naiduz, *Bases, Bullets and Ballots*, 2.

[142] Porch and Muller, "Imperial Guns Revisited," 176.

[143] Ibid, 176.

[144] Roger F. Noriega, *Plan Colombia: Major Successes and New Challenges* (Washington D.C: House International Relations Committee, May 11, 2005), 57.

for the paramilitary groups became evident. The U.S. responded by invoking the Leahy

Amendment to the Foreign Operations Act. The resulting defunding of organizations involved in

human rights violations caused the military to reduce its support for the violent groups. This in

turn led to the demobilization of 5000 paramilitary individuals from combat.[145] U.S. assistance in

support of Colombia's counter-narcotics and counter-terror operations has strengthened the

government's position, but the Uribe Administration has clearly taken responsibility and

ownership in both areas and is substantially increasing the resources committed to them while

maintaining social and economic development funding.

---

[145] Dario E. Tescher, *The Decisive Phase of Colombia's War On Narco-Terrorism* (Montgomery, AL: U.S. Air Force Counterproliferation Center, 2005), 16.

Conclusion

This paper examined three cases of military assistance advising from the end of World War II, through the Cold War, and into the Global War On Terror. The cases examined included both large and small efforts as well as an effort that transitioned over time. The research provided an analysis of the manner in which each effort accounted or failed to account for local politics and culture; what efforts were taken to shield the public from the advisory effort; whether or not the effort included any forces other than the military in the advisory effort; and the amount of training and exposure the advisor had to the supported nation in terms of length of service. While each case maintained its own nuances and combination of factors that contributed to success, as a whole, one can identify several common factors which contributed to the success of these advisory efforts.. Korea, El Salvador, and Colombia show that in fact military advisory and assistance efforts that account for local political and cultural limitations, minimize the visible public interaction between advisors and host nation personnel, include professionalization of other security forces beyond just the military, and rely on trainers with extended exposure and expertise with the host nation tend towards success. The U.S. can apply these lessons to future advisory efforts with confidence that these factors provide enduring lessons.

The three cases of U.S. military advising since the end of World War II provide a broad range of material for analysis. The Korean Military Assistance Group and the effort to assist the Republic of Korea develop its government, police, and finally military structure provides a view of a large scale advisory and assistance effort. The case is useful because it involves the opportunity to establish advisory efforts at the origin of a new state. Because of the long-term occupation of Korea by the Japanese and the subsequent partition by the victorious allies, South Korea was a nascent state despite its thousands of years of identity with the greater Korean experience. The scope and scale of this effort were vast and complicated. Its conjunction with an insurgency within the state between the various political factions, the large external threat provided by the greater Korean War, and the role that the superpower competition of the Cold

War played, created difficulties that a military advisory effort alone could not correct. By the nature of the problem, Korea required a comprehensive effort that in today's lexicon practitioners call whole of government.

The advisory effort to El Salvador also provides some unique insights. The primary lesson from the Salvadoran counterinsurgency military assistance effort is how political realities significantly frame the capability that any effort to assist another state incurs. Interstate and intrastate policy sets the stage within which military assistance and advising occurs. Additionally El Salvador provides the micro-view comparison to South Korea's macro-view of advisory efforts. Where Korea was a large and robust effort, El Salvador was very small. The context of Korea as a large-scale high intensity conflict with an ongoing insurgency where failure in either could result in the failure of the South Korean state provides one extreme, and El Salvador, where the conflict was low intensity with the insurgency remaining the principle issue reflecting the threat to the states control, provides the other. Through politically or militarily action the Salvadoran government brought the FMLN to the negotiations table, averting the challenge to the legitimacy of the state.

The final case, of Colombia, provides a useful view of how advisory efforts can change over time to adjust to changing situations within a supported state. While the effort started in the context of a Marxist insurgency, over time it evolved in a much more complex problem of a state that could not control its own territory under the peril of powerful narco-terrorist organizations that challenged the state. Over time, the lawlessness provided a greater threat to sovereignty than the insurgency, so the nature of the assistance and advising mission applied against the problem changed as well. When the U.S. feared a small insurgency inspired by the Cuban example and exacerbated by regional instability, a small scale and regional effort seemed the correct course of action to contain the problem. As the nature of the issue changed, a more nuanced military and law enforcement effort became necessary. Colombia combines El Salvador's efforts to keep the mission small with Korea's need for a large whole of government approach to solve a complex

48

and chaotic problem. Taken together, the three cases provide a useful range of examples that match the likely types of efforts that the U.S. mounts today and will likely mount in the future.

The three cases highlight the effect of local politics as well as international politics on possible solutions. Any effort that fails to account for the issues arising from local politics will likely struggle until the participants learn to adapt to them. In the Korean case, initial failures to understand politics almost led to failure when the nature of the threat changed. In El Salvador, a general understanding of the political issues helped drive the U.S. effort toward a negotiated settlement between the military government and the FMLN from the beginning, even though it took time to work through the issues to gain a detailed understanding of what mechanism that would entail. In the interim, the professionalization of the military and police provided the key stepping stones to progress. In Colombia, the U.S. understood the political issues and history behind the insurgency and designed an advisory effort to ameliorate the negative factors of the mission. As the mission changed over time, and the U.S. developed a working relationship with the host government, the U.S. government applied greater force and resources. When political factors changed, the U.S. changed its approach as well. The ramification of the political realm on the advisory effort is that such missions require at least at the administration level a direct tie-in to subject matter expertise from the U.S. State Department. The Department of State provides the resident subject matter expertise to understand the political environment and prepare the advisory effort for the political parameters within which it must operate. By the nature of the mission, all advisory missions occur under the umbrella of the interagency environment and require a whole of government approach.

Culture also plays a critical role in establishing the parameters within which an advisory effort can be successful. When the advisors fail to appreciate the culture of the supported state, they form less than optimal solutions. If the gap in understanding is significant, the solutions attempted create greater problems than those that they solve. All three cases provide examples where well-meaning advisors created issues by applying solutions that appeared logical and appropriate in the context of U.S. culture, but were ineffective or harmful when applied in another culture. The use of Japanese administrators was almost disastrous in Korea, failures to understand the linkages between paramilitary organizations and the legitimate police and military lead to human rights abuses that undermined the Salvadoran effort until the congressional action ameliorated the issue. In Colombia, the insurgents and cartels used the perception of the history of U.S. imperialistic actions throughout Latin American during the 19th and 20th century to undermine the advisory effort.

Ultimately, understanding culture requires detailed and long-term study and immersion. A dedicated cadre must provide each advisory mission with the cultural subject matter expertise to be successful. Historically this mission is performed by special forces units which are regionally aligned in conjunction with foreign area officers to provide the political-military interface. However, the increasing number and size of advisory mission since the end of the Cold War have stretched U.S. capacity to the point that non-specialized troops are performing the advisory mission. The Advise and Assist Brigade originated as an effort to overcome this shortcoming and reduce the number of troops required to both secure a state and provide an advisory effort, however, the training of advisors lacked the regional cultural expertise found in a specialized advisory unit. Another current design proposal is to regionally align BCTs to specific regions in order to develop sufficient cultural expertise over time. An alternate solution exists in individualized training that rewards soldiers for gaining and maintaining regional cultural expertise. Such a program could be managed by Human Resources Command and consist of specific regional cultural tests that are tracked in a database army wide. The program would need incentives to reward soldiers who passed the tests and manage the assignments of personnel to maximize the use of cultural expertise. A similar program already exists to track language proficiency.

In order to reduce the friction that arises from political restraints and cultural misunderstandings, advisory efforts tend to minimize interactions between the advising force and the local populations. A mechanism that advisors applied successfully in two of the three cases consisted of regionalized schools that allowed for training and advising outside of the confines of the state receiving military assistance. Such a process isolates the unit undergoing training from distractions, reduces the burden of support the nation receiving assistance must provide to the advisory effort, assists in improving relations among trained forces throughout the region, and allows the advisors to develop regionalized understanding of security issues. Minimizing interactions is much more difficult if the number of security forces available is insufficient to both execute sufficient missions to maintain a safe and secure environment and provide whole units blocks of time to conduct extended training cycles.

A consistent theme for advisory efforts since World War II is that seldom are the advisory efforts focused on the military alone. Whether advising federal police, constabulary forces, border security forces, coast guard equivalents, or the judiciary, advisory efforts that hope to tackle the complex problems of the modern state inevitably train other forces than the military alone. This fact reflects in current doctrine and practice. This is also the underlying factor behind the U.S. preference for the whole of government approach to stability operations and counterinsurgency. In order to cope with this emergent requirement, advisory efforts require interagency coordinators in the administrical level. Part of the force requirement should include personnel to manage the requisition and application of specialized trainers that the military does not possess organically.

A final factor that provides utility in successful advisory models derives from allowing the advisor extended exposure to the operating environment. Exposure provides the basis for understanding the culture and allows for the development of relationships between advisors and their counterparts so that honest exchanges of information lead to improved solutions to the root problems of the insurgency. While each of the three cases required varying lengths of service from its advisors, each show that rapid turnover of advisory force personnel is detrimental to mission accomplishment. While personnel responsible for executing soldier training may

51

successfully serve less than a year, the advisors responsible for developing leaders within organizations tend to require terms greater than a year to complete that mission. This process receives even greater enhancement if the advisor serves repeatedly within the same region, because he develops sufficient cultural expertise to enable rapid bridging of gaps in understanding and accelerated capacity to build relationships with a counterpart.

Some salient points arise from the survey of these advisory efforts. The most obvious is that each advisory mission requires tailoring to fit the culture and environment in which it must perform. Attempts at blindly implementing solutions based on previous models do not guarantee success in future operations, and are probably detrimental. A second lesson is that the size of the mission is not as critical to determining the outcome as the length of the mission. While this paper contends that keeping the size of the advisory effort as small as possible reduces some of the negative aspects of societal perception of and negative social interactions with the advising force, the advisory effort to South Korea experienced its greatest success at the same time the program was at its height of American advisors. While El Salvador and Colombia succeeded with small efforts, and South Korea succeeded with a larger one, all three took substantial time to achieve results. The third lesson is a derivative of the second. It reflects that success in military advising takes time. In Korea and El Salvador, it took about six years to establish significant reforms to correct the initial deficiencies of the security forces, and eight to ten years to bring about full success. In Colombia, the success took decades. Leaders should not expect future advisory efforts to be quick fixes to systemic problems. The fourth and final lesson is that political constraints will affect the advisory effort. These influences to the effort to advise and assist another nation's complete security apparatus require a holistic approach larger than a department of defense solution alone. Successful advisory efforts in the future will require support from many agencies with specific capabilities and areas of expertise not resident in military only efforts. These four lessons provide a useful method to conceptualize approaches to providing future military advisory missions.

BIBLIOGRAPHY

Anderson, Thomas P. *The War of the Dispossessed: Honduras and El Salvador 1969*. Lincoln, NE: University of Nebraska Press, 1981.

Bailey, Cecil E. "OPATT: The U.S. Army Advisers in El Salvador." *Special Warfare* (December 2004),18-29.

Birtle, Andrew J. *U.S. Army Counterinsurgency and Contingency Operations Doctrine 1860-1941*. Washington D.C.: United States Army Center of Military History, 2003.

_____. *U.S. Army Counterinsurgency and Contingency Operations Doctrine 1942-1976*.Washington D.C.: United States Army Center of Military History, 2007.

Boot, Max. *The Savage Wars of Peace: Small Wars and the Rise of American Power*. New York, NY: Basic Books, 2002.

Bronner, Ethan. "US aide talks of troop help for Colombia," *The Baltimore Sun* (August 21, 1989), p. 1.

Childress, Michael. *The Effectiveness of U.S. Training Efforts in Internal Defense and Development: The Cases of El Salvador and Honduras*. Santa Monica, CA: RAND National Defense Research Institute, 1995.

Cumings, Bruce. *The Origin of the Korean War*. Princeton: Princeton University Press, 1990.

Department of the Army. Field Manual (FM) 3-07.1 2009*: Security Force Assistance*. Washington, D.C.: U.S.Department of the Army, 2009.

Department of Defense. *Department of Defense Directive Number 3000.05*. Washington D.C.:Government Printing Office, November 28, 2005.

_____. Joint Publication (JP) 3-57 *Civil-Military Operations*. Washington D.C.: GovernmentPrinting Office, July 2008.

_____. *Quadrennial Defense Review Report*. Washington D.C.: Department of Defense, February 2010.

Dubey, Oeindrila, and Suresh Naiduz. *Bases, Bullets and Ballots: the Effect of U.S. Military Aid on Political Conflict in Colombia*. Working Paper 197. Washington D.C.: Center for Global Development. January 2010.

Eighth U.S. Army. *KMAG Handbook*. Eighth Army Publishing Directorate, 1953.

Evans, Michael. "War in Columbia Volume I: The Andean Strategy," National Security Archive Electronic Briefing Book No. 69.http://www.gwu.edu/~nsarchiv/NSAEBB/NSAEBB69/part1.html (accessed August 7, 2011).

_____. "War in Columbia Volume II: Counter-drug Operations," National Security Archive Electronic Briefing Book No. 69.http://www.gwu.edu/~nsarchiv/NSAEBB/NSAEBB69/part2.html (accessed August 7, 2011).

_____. "War in Columbia Volume III: Conditioning Security Assistance," National Security Archive Electronic Briefing Book No. 69.http://www.gwu.edu/~nsarchiv/NSAEBB/NSAEBB69/part3.html (accessed August 7, 2011).

Fishel, Kimbra L., and Edwin G. Corr. "UN Peace Operations in El Salvador: The Manwaring Paradigm in a Traditional Setting." in *The Savage Wars of Peace: Towards a New Paradigm of Peace Operations*, John T. Fishel ed. Boulder, CO: Westview Press, 1998.

Fleming, Adam Lum. *Colombia's Resurrection: Alternative Development is the Key to Democratic Security*. Monterey, CA: Naval Postgraduate School, 2004.

Froehlich, Dean K. *Military Advisors and Counterparts in Korea: A Study of Personal Traits and Role Behaviors*. Alexandria, Virginia: Human Resources Research Organization, 1971.

Gibby, Bryan. *Fighting in a Korean War: The American Advisory Missions from 1946-1953*. PhD Dissertation, Ohio State University, 2004.

_____."American Advisors to the Republic of Korea: America's First Committment in the Cold War, 1946-1950." In *Military Advising and Assistance: From Mercenaries to Privatization, 1815-2007*, Donald Stoker, ed. New York, NY: Routledge, 2008.

Graham, Bob, Brent Scowcroft and Michael Shifter. "Toward Greater Peace and Security in Colombia, Forging a Constructive U.S. Policy." Washington D.C.: Council on Foreign Relations, 2000.

Grimmett, Richard F. "Instances of Use of United States Armed Forces Abroad, 1798 – 2004" Congressional Research Service report RL30172. Washington D.C.: Congressional Research Service, October 2004, http://www.au.af.mil/au/awc/awcgate/crs/rl30172.htm (Accessed August 12, 2011).

Hausrath, Alfred H. *The KMAG Advisor: Role and Problems of the Military Advisor in Developing an Indigenous Army for Combat Operations in Korea*. Bethesda, Maryland: Operational Research Office, Johns Hopkins University, 1957.

Hausrath, Alfred H. and David S. Fields. *Integration of ROK Soldiers into US Army Units (KATUSA)*. Bethesda, Maryland: Operational Research Office, Johns Hopkins University, 1957.

Henelly, Michael J. "U.S. Policy in El Salvador: Creating Beauty or the Beast." *Parameters*, (Spring 1993), 59-69.

Herbst, Jeffery. *States and Power in Africa: Comparative Lessons in Authority and Control*. Princeton: Princeton University Press, 2000.

Huh, Nam-sung. *The Quest for a Bulwark of Anti-Communism: The Formation of the Republic of Korea Army Officer Corps and Its Political Socialization 1945-1950*. PhD Dissertation, Ohio State University, 1987.

Isacson, Adam. "The U.S. military in the war on drugs," in *Drugs and Democracy in Latin America: The Impact of US Policy*, C. Youngers and E. Rosin, eds, Boulder, Colorado: Lynne Rienner Publishers, 2005.

Lansing, Robert. "Memorandum by Secretary of State Robert Lansing for President Woodrow Wilson, November 24, 1915,*" Papers Relating to the Foreign Affairs of the United States: The Lansing Papers*, Vol. II. Washington, DC: Government Printing Office, 1940.

Lee, Young-Woo. *The United States and the Formation of the Republic of Korea Army 1945-1950*. Ann Arbor, Michigan: University Microfilms International, 1984.

Mahnken, Thomas G. "The Role of Advisory Support in the Long War Against Terrorist Extremist Groups." In *Security Assistance: U.S. and International Perspectives*, Kendall D. Gott and Michael G. Brooks eds., 505-518. Fort Leavenworth, KS: Combat Studies Institute Press, 2006.

54

Marks, Paul. "Joint Pub 3-07.15, Tactics, Techniques and Procedures for Advising Foreign Nationals and the American Mission". *Small Wars and Insurgencies* (Spring 2001), 31-58.

Mendel, William W. "Colombia's Threats to Regional Security," *Military Review* (May-June 2001).

Millett, Allan. *The War for Korea, 1945-1950: A House Burning*. Lawrence: University Press of Kansas, 2005.

Millett, Richard L. *Searching for Stability: the Development of U.S. Constabulary Forces in Latin America and the Philippines*. The Long War Series Occasional Paper 30. Fort Leavenworth, KS: Combat Studies Institute Press, 2010.

_____. "The Limits of Influence: Creating Security Forces in Latin America," *Joint Forces Quarterly*, No. 42 (3rd Quarter, 2006), 14–16.

Noriega, Roger F. *Plan Colombia: Major Successes and New Challenges*. Washington D.C: House International Relations Committee. May 11, 2005.

Porch, Douglas and Christopher W. Muller. "Imperial Grunts Revisited: The U.S. Advisory Mission in Colombia," In *Military Advising and Assistance: From Mercenaries to Privatization, 1815-2007*, Donald Stoker, ed. New York, NY: Routledge, 2008.

Ramsey III, Robert D. *Advise for Advisors: Suggestions and Observations from Lawrence to the Present*. The Long War Series Occasional Paper 19. Fort Leavenworth, KS: Combat Studies Institute Press, 2006.

_____. *Advising Indigenous Forces: American Advisors in Korea, Vietnam, and El Salvador*. The Long War Series Occasional Paper 18. Fort Leavenworth, KS: Combat StudiesInstitute Press, 2006.

Rempe, Dennis M. *The Past as Prologue: A History of Counterinsurgency Policy in Colombia, 1958-66*. Carlisle, PA: Strategic Studies Institute, U.S. Army War College, 2002.

Rosello, Victor M. "Lessons from El Salvador," *Parameters* (Winter 1993-1994), 100-108.

Sawyer, Robert. *Military Advisors in Korea: KMAG in War and Peace*. Washington: Office of the Chief of Military History, 1962.

Shifter, Michael. "Colombia at War," *Current History,* vol. 98 (March 1999).

Stoker, Donald. "The History and Evolution of Foreign Military Advising and Assistance, 1815-2007," In *Military Advising and Assistance: From Mercenaries to Privatization, 1815-2007*, Donald Stoker ed. New York, NY: Routledge, 2008.

Tescher, Dario E. *The Decisive Phase of Colombia's War On Narco-Terrorism*. Montgomery, AL: U.S. Air Force Counterproliferation Center, 2005.

Thucydides. *History of the Peloponnesian War*. London: Penguin Books, 1972.

Valenzuela, Alfred A. and Victor M. Rosello, "Expanding Roles and Missions in the War on Drugs and Terrorism: El Salvador and Colombia," *Military Review* (March- April 2004).

Waghelstein, John D. "Ruminations of a Wooly Mammoth, or Training and Advising in Counterinsurgency and Elsewhere During the Cold War," In *Military Advising and Assistance: From Mercenaries to Privatization, 1815- 2007*, Donald Stoker ed. New York, NY: Routledge, 2008.